When Did I Become the Enemy?

By Katrina Brooks

DORRANCE
PUBLISHING CO
EST. 1920
PITTSBURGH, PENNSYLVANIA 15238

Dorrance Publishing Co
585 Alpha Drive
Pittsburgh, PA 15238
Visit our website at *www.dorrancebookstore.com*

ISBN: 979-8-8852-7184-4
eISBN: 979-8-8852-7640-5

When Did I
Become the Enemy?

Dedication

This book is dedicated to my lifelines, my daughters Shanita,
Infinitee & Qua-Dayza & my grandson A'yaan.
"Dare to be you & still be loved!"

Thanks

Special thanks, with all my heart, & all of me I want to first thank GOD. My family & true friends. My pastors, Rev David Jefferson Sr. (My youth & teenage years) & Pastor Dr. Lawrence Powell (My young adult & present years) two men of GOD who help direct me in the right path, I thank GOD for them. My Sunday school teacher then Jeanette Tucker now I call Aunt Nette. She helped me learn the books of the Bible & understand its purpose. She will always have a special place in my heart. To all those people who saw in me what I didn't see in myself.

To my dear friend Sharon Cedeno & Cousin Nona Lomax who I can talk to with no judgment & also understand the word LOYALTY. To Diane Bryant, my mentor, my spiritual mother in Christ, who always gave her ear & lots of words of wisdom & encouragement. To each one of these people, I truly thank you, love you, appreciate you & thank GOD for you .

When did I become the enemy? What about me? How did I get here? These are all questions I used to always ask GOD. With the spirit that I have and the energy I put out into this world, I would never have believed I would be treated in any way other than that of which I have put out. I was taught to treat others how I wanted to be treated. I was taught to love unconditionally. So, what happened? Why didn't I get that?

I used to wonder why I was receiving the opposite. I was confused; I couldn't understand it. I never set out to hurt anyone. I was never spiteful to anyone, nor would I ever treat anyone bad. I stayed mindful of how I treated and spoke to people. I stayed aware of how I interacted with people. I respected everyone like a human being first. I never treated anyone less than a human being. Titles came secondary to me; I respected that in the latter. I would never mistreat anyone, and especially not the ones I love. I don't even like to be upset at anyone. I'm human, so I do get upset, but not for long. I always promised myself not to stay in that space too long.

I don't feel right being mad. I'm not an angry person, so therefore I'm never angry. I pray to GOD and let things go, and I don't hold grudges. I would never totally curse anyone out in a disrespectful manner. I don't even like to curse. When I do curse, it makes me feel so guilty, I regret it the second I let it out my mouth. I ask GOD to forgive me and help me with this ugly habit because I truly want to stop. I know I can stop cursing; I have done it before in the past. I went two years without cursing—it seemed easy at the time, but now... I don't know how easy it's going to be.

I know you're probably asking, "Well, what happened?"

Life! That's what happened, haha. As I got older and started experiencing life and the different people in it, my cursing came back and started flowing out frequently. Dealing with people with their different personalities and different issues can do that to you... (have you cursing, that is!). It can be hard not to curse now but because I want to stop again, I try my hardest not to say a bad word. The line of work that I am in is very challenging. My businesses are even challenging.

The difficult people I come across aren't a challenge for me too much because I believe GOD equipped me for it. Dealing with difficult people and their feelings challenges me to be disciplined, and that discipline helps me to not curse during those difficult interactions. GOD is helping me to be mindful not to curse. The fact that I stay professional when dealing with people prevents me from cursing. I have a calm demeanor and always try to make the best out of all situations, no matter how bad. I tend to give people too much benefit of the doubt.

I'm not one to panic, no matter the circumstances. I'm one of the most positive people you'll ever meet. I have a pure heart and want the best for others. I thank no one but GOD for that. There was a time I didn't understand why people panic. My thing was always: If there's a problem, find the solution. That simple.

As I became a young adult and a parent at a young age, I started taking life more seriously. I put my kids first, other people, then GOD. As I got older and understood that GOD was all I needed, I then put Him first, then my kids, then others. As you can see, I never put myself into the equation. I always put myself last. I've made sacrifices for others because I watch my mother, my aunts, and grandmothers make sacrifices for others. I was intrigued by that. I thought that was the most important part of life: helping others; sacrificing for others. (As I learned later, many in the Bible felt that way as well.)

I remember asking GOD to send a person like me to come into my life; a person with similar personality, heart, and spirit.

I did have some great people come into my life, but not many who had the personality or spirit as I have. I prayed this prayer for years, believing GOD would answer my prayer one day. I always say, "I don't know how, but I know HE will one day." I always believed that whatever I asked GOD, for He would deliver. He has shown up and showed out for me time and time again with many blessings after blessings in my life.

I didn't know early on in my life that I had to learn to completely lean on GOD. I had to learn and understand how let go and let GOD completely. I had to stop just saying it and truly let Him take over all aspects of my life. I seen it for myself that when I did it my way, it didn't work out well for me. When I half gave it to GOD and thought I should step in and help Him out, it didn't work in my favor. It took years before I learned to completely let it all go and give it to GOD. I learned that He could do it better than I ever could, and He does NOT need my help.

Years ago, I had a best friend to break my heart. She cut me completely off, and I didn't know why. I kept reaching out to her to get answers but received no response. Sadly enough, after a year and a half later, I received an answer and the answer made me go from hurt to mad. The answer she gave me was that she felt I was replacing her with new friends I just had met. I was floored by this. This was a friendship of over 10 years. We cried, prayed, partied, and even at one point worked together. She knew me better than most. Most people who know me and are around me know for sure I'm going to make sure everyone around me is good. I make sure if you're at my home, you're comfortable; I cater to everyone, but new guests get extra special treatment. She knew this about me, so how could she say she thought I was replacing her? How could she just cut me off completely for THAT reason?

I was just coming to acceptance with the fact that she cut

me off, so when she called me with that reason, I became upset. It didn't sound right. It did not sit well with me that a best friend could do this. This was someone I shared a special bond with; someone I called my best friend, my sister. It took me a while to get over that entire situation. No one knew I was going through this. I just fasted and stayed in prayer. GOD started healing my heart, helping me to understand what was happening and helping me to come into acceptance with it all, so I could move on. It wasn't easy because it didn't make sense.

I learned that, in life, a lot of things won't make sense. I had to learn to just come into acceptance with whatever came my way, good or bad. That situation made me put a wall up. I never got close to many female friends ever again. When did I become the enemy?

In my early adult years, I had a lot of female friends who all changed as I got older and wiser. I used to always entertain at my home and invited all my friends and family. No one had to bring anything; I cooked plenty of food and had plenty of drinks. I did dinner parties for years. After a while, those same friends (I thought were friends) would have parties and not invite me. A part of me was upset because I never left them out; they were always at my functions. The other part of me knew I no longer wanted to be around people like this anymore. I knew I was outgrowing them anyway. When did I become the enemy?

A few years ago, I had a co-worker who I rode to work with in her car at least once a week cut me off as well. She would pick me up from my second job (part-time job) to take me to work at our full-time job. I let my boyfriend at the time use my car (another sacrifice), so she would pick me up. I appreciated her and would never take anything or anyone for granted.

One day, we were headed out to go to a flea market on a Saturday. I drove to her house and parked my car, and from there, we got in her vehicle to head out to the flea market. On our way there, she needed to stop at the bank. On our way out of the bank, she and another car ran into each other. Nothing major, I thought at the time. Neither of us went to hospital, but as usual, we were sore later on that night. She asked me that day would I sue her, and I told her no. That wasn't a thought in my mind. I was just happy we all were okay.

Two weeks later, on an early Saturday morning, I woke up in the most pain I ever felt... yes, even worse than contractions. I didn't know what was happening. I couldn't move. I crawled to my bedroom door to call my daughter to call my neighbor at the time, who called the ambulance. Once at the hospital, they ran tests and gave me all types of pain medications, which none worked. I later found out that I had three herniated disks in my neck. I had to have surgery. At that time, I rejected the surgery because of how they explained the procedure to me. They would have to cut the front of my neck and go in through there to get to the disks. A few weeks of holding my arm up for relief and taking lots of pain meds, I finally agreed to the surgery.

I told my friend about the pain I was having, and because she didn't have the same pain, she started telling people I was faking, so I could sue her, and she stopped speaking to me. I still had no intentions of suing her. I just wanted to be relieved of the pain I was in. I ended up getting one of the three disks replaced. Because this was a permanent injury, all they could do was help me with some relief from the pain. By these three disks being injured, it caused my right arm, hand, and fingers to be numb, and my fingers keep a sharp stinging pain in them. The other procedure I had to do was get a nerve stimulator implanted in my back. I sent her pictures of the implant and explained to her that I wasn't faking, and this was nothing I would wish on anyone. She never responded; she was still telling people I was going to sue her.

This was about four to five years ago. Still to this day, she has not spoken to me, and still to this day, I never sued her, and still to this day, I walk around with a stimulator implanted in my back and my right side numb. (I'm right-handed.) No one would ever know this because I never talk about it, and I don't complain. I learned to live with the pain. I don't let the pain get me down. There are days when the pain is unbearable, but I still push through.

How can people be so selfish? I will never know. I don't have a selfish spirit. She never reached out to me to see if I was okay. She stopped speaking to me because she thought I was going to sue her, and I never did. When did I become the enemy?

Even my kids' fathers didn't do right by me. I raised my daughters alone for the most part. One thing I did not do was close the door on them as dads. I never talked bad about them to their daughters. How my daughters feel about their dads today is because of the parts their dads played in their lives. Even when I was married, I felt like a single mom. I believe that I am the dream wife. I am old-school; I catered to my husband; cooked, cleaned, and loved him unconditionally. The home front was always taken care of. I won't go into detail as to how they wronged me, but I would say my daughters are their only daughters, their princesses, and I couldn't understand then how they could neglect our girls. My dad had 10 kids, and he spent time with us all, and we all have stories and memories of our dad that we can talk about for days. My girls don't have that and will never have it. When did I become the enemy?

The title of this book came to me over 20 years ago. I felt I was pouring so much of me and my love into others and not getting anything back. I understood that what you do for others is between me and GOD. I knew that anything you did for others, you shouldn't expect back from them. I used to question GOD, "What about me?" I couldn't understand how I was showing people so much love and treating them with so much respect, but I was being treated like an enemy from these same people I showered with love. I asked GOD, "What am I doing wrong?" I love unconditionally; that's how I was taught to love. I treated people too well because that's how I wanted to be treated. The results of my actions seemed to cause people to resent me, be spiteful towards me, treat me bad, talk about me, and even call me "extra," saying I was doing too much.

Some even said I had motives behind my acts of kindness. I felt like, instead of them looking at me as the genuine, loving person that I am, they looked at me as an enemy. I say enemy because of their actions towards me. While I was showing them so much love, they were spitefully doing evil things to me. I thought to myself, *How can anyone treat someone who loves them unconditionally so bad?*

It took me years of heart breaks, hurt feelings, and disappointments to finally learn why I was being treated this way by the people I love and did the most for. The blessing that came out of this treatment is that I got a closer walk with GOD. My relationship with Him grew stronger as I turned to Him for answers. I prayed more and listened to the Word more, which helped me emotionally cope with feeling rejected and treated like an enemy. Getting discouraged is easy, especially when the letdown comes from the people you love or you have been loyal to. I had to learn to use that energy as fuel to push through and motivate myself. To have the ones I love disrespect me, call me names, do spiteful things to me, and even make things up about me was a hard pill to swallow.

Today, I Am Loving

Who am I? I am the daughter of the Most High. Born and raised in Elizabeth, NJ, I moved away to raise my daughters in a better environment. I learned along the way that you must remove yourself and your kids from places and people you outgrow or don't mean you any good. When I was growing up in Elizabeth, it was an extended family environment. Everyone family knew each other one way or another. There was some respect back then. As I got older and had kids, that generation not only didn't respect other adults, but they also barely respected their own parents. I didn't want my children in that toxic environment. I wanted to show them that there were other places outside of Elizabeth. I took my children places to show them there were beautiful places outside the city of Elizabeth and state of New Jersey. I instilled in them the morals and values my elders instilled in me.

To walk in the spirit and not the flesh is something I work on every day. I feed my spirit every day. I choose to starve my flesh. It's nothing I have mastered yet; I'm still working on this. To turn to the spirit when I'm being attacked has become an easy task for me now. It's something I didn't know was an option for me growing up. I heard about it, but never put it into play until now. To be everything to a person who attacks you is hard. It's only the power of GOD that helps me. I can give that credit to no one else.

How can we continue to love the ones who break our heart? How can we feed and continue to nurture the ones who betray us? Prayer keeps me sane. Prayer takes me from not being angry to remaining calm. Prayer allows me to continue to stay in the spirit when I'm feeling my human side trying to take over. It is not normal for someone to hurt you and act like they didn't, then think everything is okay. It's not easy to turn the other cheek; it is not normal that someone disrespect you, and you pray for them; it is not normal that someone put their hands on you, and you spare them. None of this is normal human behavior.

I know GOD has His hands on me. It's not me; I'm not soft, and I'm no body's punk. My head hurts plenty of nights because my flesh is wrestling with my spirit. For someone to stay around you and act like they did nothing to you can drive you crazy. To put everything in GOD's hands and think GOD isn't moving fast enough isn't easy, asking GOD why He keeps letting these things happen to you when you're doing everything you're supposed to do—or at least trying to do everything right.

Keeping your faith in the midst of all this is a heck of a

task for anyone. You must continue to stay in prayer. Listen to the Word, listen to gospel music... anything else will land you in jail. You can't take things into your own hands. You can't give the adversary the satisfaction of you losing your mind. You can't let the adversary take you off your focus in life. That's all it is. The adversary knows your worth; they know GOD has His hands on you. They know GOD is going to take you to higher and higher levels. The adversary knows you are a chosen one. We must learn and acknowledge it for ourselves; once we learn it, we have to act accordingly. We must walk according to GOD's will for our lives.

Once I started understanding why GOD allowed me to go through the things I went through, it became easier to tolerate the people I was around, and staying calm and not feeding into distractions of the adversary came easier. I will never tell anyone that taking abuse is easy. Whether it's verbal, physical, or emotional, it's not; it's a horrible feeling, especially because it's coming from the people you love.

Having faith in people around you who don't even have faith in themselves isn't easy either. Without GOD's help guiding me, I don't know where I would be. Let me correct that: I do know where. I would be in a mental institution, dead or in jail. That's reality. I know I don't look like what I've been through; I don't carry myself like what I've been through. I don't entertain what I've been through. I don't walk like what I've been through. I don't talk like what I've been through. I don't act like what I've been through. I walk, talk, and carry myself like the child of GOD I am. I never let those people who tried to break me change who I am. I would never let those things that attacked me dictate who I am, make me act out of character, or make me stoop to their level. That's not what GOD wants for me. This is what I know; this is what I keep in my mind, and this is why I'm able to not react to every attack.

GOD said He will fight my battles. Who am I to dispute that? I've seen it done on several occasions. GOD said, "Touch not my anointed." At some point, I realized I was anointed; I had to be. To be such an amazing person in general—a great dependable friend, sister, mother, girlfriend, wife, daughter, and employee—and still get attacked by the same people who I have been there for no matter what, yes, it hurts. It hurt like heck.

To be betrayed by the ones you love is disappointing. To see the selfishness in the ones you stuck your neck out for is nauseating. To be disrespected by the ones you care about is disgusting. To be degraded by the ones you motivate and help elevate is painful. There are so many questions that come into your mind when these things are happening; there're so many scenarios that come into your mind of how you want things to play out. In order to remain sane and deal with this, you have to go into prayer. You have to get into the spirit. I learned to get out of my feelings and into the spirit... how necessary that is! It helps so much.

GOD will reveal to you the answers to every question. He will give you the strength you need in that moment to get through that situation. He will give you the comfort you need at that time. You can't be so angry that you don't seek Him at these times. These are the times you need Him most. Reality is, if you allow yourself to deal with these people on your own terms in your own way, it's not going to end well. God's plan is better than ours. He can do it better than we can. Although we want rapid results, He knows best, and His timing is right on time. If we do it ourselves, we will mess ourselves up trying to get revenge.

Revenge, evil for evil, spitefulness, or vindictiveness are no spirits of mine, and never will be. I take my walk with GOD very seriously. Those around me know I do. I'm not a hypocrite, nor do I act "holier than thou." I stick to my morals and values that were instilled in me as a child. I am still a work in progress and won't allow anyone or anything to distract me from it. GOD's grace is what's been carrying me, and I'm not ever letting that go. Too many people take life and the people and things in their life for granted.

GOD knows and sees it all. Most people are getting the beat down of their life on the inside and portraying something else on the outside. We can tell by the way they talk and treat other people. Although these things were happening to me, I was never bitter, angry, miserable, or evil. I never treated these people back the same way they treated me. I never treated anyone else badly because I was being attacked. The statement remains: True "misery loves company." The adversary didn't like my spirit, so he used these people to try to break me down. It's not easy trying to explain to people you love that they're being used by the adversary to attack you. They'll look at you like you have five heads, and some you just can't tell at all because they'll never believe you. The ones who knew they were being used sometimes still didn't try to fight those spirits with me. They still came against me because to them it was easier. You can't make someone believe that they're being used to attack you, and it's not always the adversary using them. Sometimes it's just them; they are the adversary. We have to come into acceptance with what it is. We can't sugar coat it or make excuses for them. Call it how you see it because it is what it is. At that point, it's up to you how you deal with them. Me personally want to keep them out my space.

I have no problem with loving people from afar. I take my smiles and positive energy seriously. My smiles are genuine: I don't have to fake a smile; it's part of my make up. If I can't smile around someone, I don't want to be around them. My positive energy will not be compromised by negative energy. I pray; I read the Word; I sing and listen to encouraging, motivational people, songs, and spiritual words. I keep candles burning; I burn sage, and I spray down my house with spiritual cleansing sprays to help keep my home clear of negativity and help keep my energy and spirits uplifted. Of course, there're days I wake up feeling *blah*, but after my prayer call or a quick prayer, my spirits are back uplifted. A conversation with my Heavenly Father usually does it for me.

We cannot let the adversary make us feel defeated at any level of our life when our FATHER already told us we were victorious. He already won our battles and went on home. Why are we feeling the need to fight? Yes, our flesh takes us there, but we have the power to back out of that ring we have no business being in, especially if it's a recurring battle. Some of us get taken down the same road by the same people several times. I know I have. That's that giving people "the benefit of doubt" I was talking about. We have to know better than to entertain that same person with the same issue. They're not satisfied with themselves, so they want to keep taking you there. NOPE! GOD didn't tell us to keep fighting any battles He already won. Tell that person that; let them know. Scream the Word at them; call on Jesus, and they'll stop. It's mentally, physically, and spiritually draining. Once I learned, I let the adversary know he will never break me; he will never have me out my character, nor will he ever have me change who my GOD ordained me to be.

I learned to concentrate on my lane. Everything I have on my goals list for me or for my daughters and now my grandson is all I want to focus on. With GOD first and His hand on my life, I know I can't fail. When I'm focused, the attacks come so hard. Attacks can make you say later for it all because you get tired of constantly fighting off these attacks. It's totally draining. The attacks come as a distraction to take you off course. Don't let nothing or no one trick you out your position. Your number one position is as a child of GOD who GOD sent here for a purpose; to do His assignment, spread His love and His word. For me, over time, it has gotten easier to ignore the attacks and send them back to where they came from only because I'm more in the Word these days than I ever been.

One thing I've learned is the attacks never stop. We learn to deal with them. Biggie said it best: "More money, more problems." I also heard it said, "Different levels, different devils!" Truly knowing and believing GOD to handle them gives me a peace of mind. I don't worry about the attacks anymore. I stay fasting and prayed up and ready for them. I give them to GOD and keep moving. Every day I thank GOD for preparing me for such a day as this.

All my life I felt shortchanged by those who should value me the most. I met strangers who cling to me the moment they come in contact with me with no issues. While those who know me well "choose" to shortchange me. Rather, it's shortchanging me on love, friendship, or even value; it's hurtful because these are the same people I would have given my last dollar to or even given my life for.

It's disappointing that my loved ones and those close to me treated me this way. I have let people borrow my last and never seen it again. I didn't know then that what you let people borrow, don't expect it back, but why would someone not want to pay back what was given to them to borrow? What makes someone feel like you don't need your money back? I know this is why I'm blessed beyond measures. With GOD's grace and a lot of prayer, I've forgiven these people and have gotten through those nauseating moments and still love these people the same. To me, these people feel like you don't deserve what you worked so hard for, your money, or even your own time to yourself. I re-member going to school and working two jobs while raising my daughters. I had studying to do, housework to do, job work to do, and people still called on me to help them with something, never once asking me how I'm doing or how my kids are doing; just asking me for favors.

When did I become the enemy?

Most of those same people who did you wrong are sitting back waiting for you to do something back to them; meaning get revenge or treat them the way they treated you. I was told this by someone. They said they're just sitting back waiting for me to get them back. I said my mind isn't even on that. I'm not even thinking of doing anything bad to anyone. My GOD didn't give me a spirit of revenge; my GOD would be upset with me if I did that. I'm not blocking my blessing to give someone else the satisfaction of wanting me to stoop to their level. I never will do what someone else did to me if I never had the desire to do it before. Don't allow no one to take you there. Let them be raggedy on their own, and let GOD deal with them and their actions. Don't give any energy to irrelevant non-factors. That's not for us to do.

GOD said, "Vengeance is mine." Some men do things to women that most women would never do to men, and as we know, most won't handle it the same way that a woman handled it. Women who treat other women bad are the same; they can dish it out but can't take it. It's something in them that makes them treat other women like that. Real women can get along. The lie that we can't isn't true. Yes, there are some who can't, but that's because they are still immature and have issues with themselves, so they look as to other women as a threat and take their issues out on the other women.

If we seek GOD at any time in life, He will heal us; heal our hearts and spirits. He told us to forgive. He'll direct us and change our worldly way of thinking. GOD doesn't want us to be against each other. Throughout the Bible, He says love each other, love one another, love your mother, your father, your sisters and brothers—that's all of us. My heart is pure, and I am able to love everyone. It comes easy for me; it comes naturally. I know how to love and to forgive. I'm still learning other areas, but I've mastered these two areas.

I'm going to say again: Don't get tricked out your position. It's easier to get off track, but it's rewarding to stay focused. My Father owns the world. If you focus and make sacrifices, it's well worth it in the end.

Now I know at the end of it all, peoples' opinions don't matter. All I want to hear from my Father in Heaven is, "Well done, good and faithful servant."

There's no value to a pure heart.

GOD will never let bad get the final say.

I don't need to be connected to the people high up... I'm connected to the Most High.

When did I become the enemy?

You vs. Me… Why?

You vs. me… why? I've been everything and some to a lot of people; never changed on anyone, and always gave a thousand percent of me to anyone who needed me. I've let people live with me who felt they didn't have to pay me any rent, and I was okay with that. They ate the food I brought for the house without caring if me or my kids ate. I've taken hits for others that they would never do for me. Why would someone take that for granted?

I for you, you for me; together we are one. That's a beautiful statement I once used. When I encounter a genuine person, I know right away. most people do. Sometimes people pretend so well that you don't see their other side for a long time. As we know, all masks fall off eventually, and we get to see the true person underneath the mask. I could never understand why someone who knows they're not right would want to be around a person who is. Why play on someone's intelligence? Why play on their kindness? Why play the role?

There's something to be said about a person who can treat someone bad purposely. One thing I know is that GOD sees it all; He sees what we are all doing. He will handle it in His timing. With His grace, I was able to learn this in advance and understand it. People don't believe that we reap what we sow, good or bad. Some know and still don't care because what they reaped isn't enough to humble them yet. Eventually it will all catch up to them. You can't treat people bad and expect a good life; it just doesn't work that way. I've seen people reap what they've sown. I've also reaped what I've sown, good and bad.

FOCUSED and DETERMINED

I am a chosen one. That's why they mistreated me. GOD has a calling on my life, and I didn't belong around those people. Look at the bigger picture; don't cry. When they betrayed you, it doesn't matter. When they lied on, talked about, rejected you, and laughed at you, it doesn't matter. Look at you now. I wasn't supposed to fit in.

No eye has seen, no ear has heard, and no mind has imagined what GOD has prepared for those who love Him. But GOD has revealed these things to us by His Spirit.

There's no cockiness; there's no conceitedness; I'm only convinced and confident I will get everything my heart desires that's in alignment with GOD's will for my life. I have no reason not to believe so. I put GOD first; I treat people how GOD told me to despite how they treat me. I pay my tithes, take my communion, pray, and fast. So, the smile on my face every day is me waiting on my many miraculous blessings.

I get upset at things and people, but I don't stay there; I know better. I'm not an angry person, so you'll never see that spirit from me. My prayer life keeps me sane and humbled. Most things most people get upset about, I can smile about. Most things people think about, I don't because I know better. I keep my thinking according to what I want in my life. Yes, I'm human and crazy thoughts enter my mind, but I don't allow them to stay there. I'll pray, listen, put a word on, I'll start singing, I'll put music on any positive distraction from that thought helps.

I have no desire to consume my mind with mean thoughts of others. If GOD puts someone on my mind heavy, I'll pray for them then reach out to them see if they are okay. I don't have the spirit to talk about anyone. If you did something to me, I may vent about it and let it go. To dwell on anything longer than we should isn't mentally healthy for anyone. I stay mindful of this, so I act accordingly. I also know to keep something bottled in for so long isn't good for you either. It'll end up coming out on the wrong person. Best thing to do is address it with that person or GOD. Do not hold it in and let it fester; it's no good. I used to do that to keep the peace. I'd rather not discuss what was going on with me to avoid hearing arguments and lies.

Most people will never admit to treating you badly. They'll either justify it or just make you feel crazy for even knowing what they were trying to do to you, meaning you're not supposed to know that they're treating you wrong, so when you are calling them out on it, they call you crazy. They try to make you feel like what you're knowing they do to you isn't what it is. No one gets to tell me how to feel after they did me wrong. First thing people say is, "You're overthinking it, that's not what it is." Meanwhile I'm feeling upset not them, and they're telling me how to feel. How do they know how I should feel? They're the ones who put me in this space with their messed-up treatment, now telling me not to be upset.

Mishandled

Don't accept anything you don't want in your life.

I separated myself from people for this exact reason. If you were brought up a certain way and someone violates your morals and values, stay away from them. I learned the hard way it's okay to love from a distance. I was always available and catering to everyone else. When I stopped and realized how burnt out I was from doing this, I fell back, slowed down, and even stopped doing so much for others. It's amazing how people change on you and react and treat you differently when you become unavailable for them and no longer cater to their needs. They don't care about what you have going on in your life as long as you were there for them. It's truly a hurting feeling when the same people you catered to turn on you because you decide to put yourself into the equation and take care of yourself for a change. I watched a few people develop whole personality changes on me. I heard it in their voices (yes, the voices changed, too! Haha)—those high, excited voices I used to get became deep and dry. I still am there for them, just in my own way and on my own time. I know my purpose on this Earth, and being used and abused isn't it.

Praying to GOD for strength through every obstacle in life will have you out your feelings. I will never say you won't ever get your feelings hurt again, but you won't be so disappointed; you won't feel so let down. GOD gives you this amazing strength to deal with people and their mess. When people come up against me now, I say: "That's about right..." I know better now. I know I'm no one's enemy. I now know why people treat me the way they do, so now I react differently. I can easily nix people's mess off. When GOD revealed to me why I was treated like an enemy, I learned how to handle my feelings. For those people who treated me badly, it's not for me to deal with them. GOD said he'd fight our battles. I constantly tell myself not to get in the ring with nonsense; let whoever say whatever. I protect my space and sanity and stay far away from drama and drama-starting people. I find it sad to see so many people my age still mixed up in drama or still starting or even talking about it. I will NOT give any unnecessary drama my energy. If GOD said He got it, I'm staying out of it. This wasn't easy for me to do before because I felt I had to take up for myself and prove who I was. Now I know at 45, I don't. I don't and won't prove myself to anyone who already knows me. GOD already showed them who I was, and that's why they felt the need to try to belittle me, humiliate me, or disrespect me to others. I'm not ever worried about this anymore, or about being called names because GOD has and will handle those people His way.

I know I can't do it better than GOD. I know His plan is better than mine. I know to sit and be still; I know to be quiet and let GOD deal with them GOD's way. Trust me, they know it's GOD doing it. Whether they believe in GOD or karma or nothing at all, they know when GOD is giving them the beat down of their lives. The way GOD does it, there's no confusion whatsoever.

I now concentrate on my lane, knowing my Father owns the world. People have no idea what I endured in my lifetime, but they still want what I have and hate on me… why? I was a single mom raising three daughters, working two jobs and going to school, been married divorced and in good and bad relationships. I've been in a car accident that caused me to lose feeling in my right side. Still today I have a nerve stimulator in my back. I've had this in for four years, still moving around working, cleaning, cooking, and yes, even helping others. Most wouldn't know because I never complain or talk about it, and the ones who do know say they forget I even have it. I've always had to stay strong for my daughters. I didn't and still don't want them to want for anything. I had them; they're mine, and I want to give and show them the world was always my mindset.

I fought for many relationships but found that I was the only one fighting.

Quiet, Laid Back, and Reserved

Turn your pain into power. Sit back and watch your blessings pour in. Are you willing to give up what you know is hurting you for what's on the other side of that the unknown?

I used to be quiet and humble because I shielded myself to keep the peace. One day, GOD said, "Let the folk know how I take care of you. Let them know your story tell it all. You don't have to worry about them talking about you or criticizing this book. This is your story: they can't tell you what to write; they didn't experience this you did." This is my truth to tell.

I was thinking it was going to sound like I was looking to put people on blast and tell what I did for people. GOD said HIS true followers will get it; the rest doesn't matter. It's about treating people well despite them treating you badly. With GOD's grace and hand in my life, I will stand tall and not break. These people tried to break me while I was helping them and building them up. What I learned from this is that no matter how good you are to people, most will not appreciate it. I also learned that you can't expect you from someone else.

I know that with GOD on my side, the rest doesn't matter. When staying in the Word of GOD we can endure and conquer it all. When you decide to walk in your purpose, the adversary sends all types of attacks through any shape, form, or fashion. Jump over those hurdles, and don't stop—don't give up—keep pushing through! Pray and ask GOD for strength and guidance. He's going to get us through the attacks and show us that it's Him. You'll see that it's nobody but GOD. The way HE shows up and shows out for you will have you in awe at first. Once you continually see His work, you'll just smile and laugh. I always say, "GOD, I see you!" Haha. Another one of my sayings is: "Watch my GOD work."

My Father owns the world; I have nothing to worry about. He's carried me this far; He's going to carry me even further... no doubt in my mind.

GODfidence: Many Inflictions of the Righteous

Pray in the car, in the shower, in a quiet, peaceful space. Listen for His guidance.

Open up. Let GOD into your heart, mind, soul, and spirit. Allow Him in, and He will make you feel better in that moment you need Him. Call on His name; it will give you the strength and comfort you need.

GOD will never leave us hanging. He's a man of his word

he will never leave you nor forsake you. He will never change on you. He will give you everything he has promised. He's waiting on you to turn to Him. We are all here on assignment, so tap into it, and HE will guide you through. Even I feared my calling. When you start to see your purpose and understand it, I won't sugarcoat it at all, it's scary to step into your assignment. You must tap into it and let everything else go. You must establish that relationship with GOD for yourself and understand it in your own way.

Although I heard others talk about GOD growing up and just went off what others said, it's a different feeling to read, learn, and understand the Word for yourself. You become this other person who's been deep down inside; a better version of you. A few people will be shocked, but a lot won't be. Crazy part is, most saw it in you before you ever knew—that's why they tried to come for you. But GOD kept you covered.

Can't mess up my alignment, messing with folks trying to take revenge. GOD never said take revenge—HE said, "Vengeance is Mine." He said the battle is His. GOD can do it better than we can. GOD see it all; He sees the people who came against me. I've witnessed His work. I learned to sit back and chill and let Him handle it. GOD continues to pay me back for all I've lost and all that was taken from me, and contrasting how much people have used me, He's given me more than double for my troubles.

You must understand the love GOD has for you. He won't let these people get away with hurting you after He sees how you blessed them mightily. Do not change who you are because of how you're treated.

I Pray this book touch & Bless at least one person reading this.

Thank you all for your support.

The next few pages are songs and scriptures I listened to and read daily that helped me get through obstacles and hurdles in my life. They helped me & I pray they'll help you too. I pray and thank GOD for each one of the artist and their songs.

Songs

Open My Heart
The Battle Is Not Yours
I'm Gonna Be Ready
Order My Steps
Deliver Me
Jesus Is Real
The Blood Will Never Lose Its Power
Holy Spirit, Fall Down on Me
No Weapon Formed Against Me Shall Prosper
Because of Who You Are
Praise Is What I Do
I Told the Storm
Safe in His Arms
I Just Want to Praise You
No Greater Love
Faithful Is My GOD
The Presence of the Lord Is Here
Thank You, LORD
My Name Is Victory
It's Working
Be Blessed
Never Give Up
I Smile
I Sing Because I'm Happy
Father, Can You Hear Me?
Oh, It Is Jesus
Turning Around

Donnie McClurkin, Live from London Album

Marvelous, by Walter Hawkins
My GOD Is Awesome
Center of My Joy
Yes Lord
Let the Church Say AMEN
I Won't Complain
Something About the Name of Jesus
Grateful
I Need You to Survive
God Favored Me
I Give Myself to You
Never Would Have Made It
He Seen the Best in Me
Stand
Take Me to the King

Scriptures

Psalm 23

Psalm 91

Psalm 35

Psalm 64

Isaiah 54:17

Matthew 6:9-13

Ephesians 6:10-18

Mathew 6:33

Hebrews 11:1

Romans 8:28

Philippians 4:13

John 14:16

Proverbs 3:5-6

1 Thessalonians 5:18

Philippians 4:6-7

Psalm 119:105

Ephesians 4:32

Psalm 46:10

Jeremiah 29:11

John 3:16